101 Quick and Easy Confidence Quotes.

GW00393961

Dedications and Special Thanks.

*

I would like to dedicate this book to every person who has ever struggled or is currently struggling with their confidence and self-esteem because I am living proof that you can turn your life around, you can build your confidence and be the person you have always dreamed of being.

I grew up with very little confidence and it wasn't until my early twenties that I decided that things had to change and I fought my way to where I am today so I hope this book and these quotes can be an inspiration to you and become part of your journey to wherever you decide to take your life.

*

I also want to give Special thanks to my friends and family who have been a constant part of my journey but especially to Laverne and Tatlyn whose support of my hopes and dreams is unconditional and has never wavered. You have both been there through the ups and downs and listened to every crazy idea that I have ever had (which is a lot). Without the two of you this book and the ones that will follow would not have been possible and for that I cannot tell you how eternally grateful I am. You will always have a place in my heart but I know that you know that which is what true friendship and family is all about. Love always. Tony.

101
Quick and Easy
Confidence
Quotes.

Tony T Robinson.

Foreward.

*

Firstly, I would like to begin by saying Thank You. Thank you for purchasing this book and for taking the time to read it which I hope you will do many many times.

I put this book together with the sole purpose of inspiring other people (namely you) to be the best version of yourself that you can be.

I know that if you are reading this book you have the belief and the desire to be more than who you feel you are right now. I also know that deep down you believe and I mean truly believe that you should be living the life you have dreamed of and you should be living it your way without anxiety or fear of rejection without worrying what other people will think or say about the choices you make, without self-criticism and most certainly without that nagging little voice on your shoulder that is always telling you that you are not good enough that you will never be able to "do it" and that the world is just waiting for you to fail and fall flat on your face.

How do I know that you feel that way? I know that because that's exactly how I used to think and feel and I will let you into a secret, it's not just you and I who feel that way. On some level, to one degree or another that is how every single person on the planet feels or has felt at one time in their life, so you are not alone.

The next time you feel shy, awkward, embarrassed or think that everyone is secretly criticising you know that they too probably have the same thoughts and insecurities that you do only you don't know that is what they are thinking about themselves, so if you cannot tell what they are thinking or feeling how can they know what your insecurities and fears are?

That was a lesson that took me many years to learn. What I also came to realise was that in the same way I didn't know their thoughts and feelings they couldn't tell mine either. We are not made of glass, we are not transparent and our doubts and fears are not written in bold across our foreheads for the rest of the world to read even though if often feels that way, so you no longer need to feel intimidated and embarrassed to speak to people, you don't need to feel afraid to try something new or follow your dreams.

I have studied psychology and psychodynamic psychotherapy and the one thing that I have learned is that at a core level we are all the same. We all want and need to be liked and loved and anyone who says they don't are just too scared to admit it.

We all hurt in the same way, we all feel let down and betrayed by other people and somehow we find a way to blame ourselves for the actions of others.

We all want to be happy but yet somehow we are determined to let fear and anxiety get in the way of that happiness. We convince ourselves that we are "Not good ENOUGH" and then because we have convinced ourselves of that so called fact we start to live our lives accordingly.

We all have hopes and dreams but yet never trust ourselves enough to make those dreams a reality, instead we live a life of excuses and "Yeah buts" and then convince ourselves that we don't have the confidence, the skills, the knowledge, the luck, the money, the whatever it is you use as an excuse to prevent yourself from achieving your potential and living a life without limits, but the truth is you do have the ability, you just haven't learnt to believe in yourself yet.

Once again I can say this with a fair amount of certainty because I have lived that life and I spent a long time trying to figure out what my issues were and how to deal with them, and on many levels in many ways I have, but don't get me wrong I am not perfect by any means and I still have doubts and insecurities like everyone else but the difference is I no longer allow them to have control in my life and prevent me from doing the things I believe I should be doing and step by step day by day I am working towards fulfilling my dreams and becoming the person I know that I can and should be which is precisely why I decided to help other people build their confidence.

Once I realised that I could and did change, that I no longer needed to be held back by crippling fears and doubts and that I could step into the person I had always dreamed of being I understood that my purpose in life was to help other people do exactly the same thing because if I can do it I know that you can do it!

If I can go from being shy and insecure to training to be a counsellor/therapist to writing books and coaching people both on line and one to one then I know that you too can achieve your dreams and reach your maximum potential to be able to look fear in the face and carry on regardless. I can guarantee that with each step you take forward your confidence will increase and it will carry you through life's trials and tribulations to a destination of your choosing.

Part of my journey was to write about how people can build their confidence which I began doing through social media sites until eventually I realised that I could put my thoughts together in one place. I had always wanted to write books but the path of traditional publication is a difficult one to say the least but with today's technology we no longer need to be confined by what someone else deems as publishable or profitable and so I decided it was time to self-publish. It was time to practice what I preached. I knew in my heart that I could no longer just tell other people what they needed to do to improve their lives I had to start doing the same and with that the idea for this book was born.

I had been writing my own quotes for some time and they were very popular, I received such positive feedback from people that I decided to put them together and create 101 Quick and Easy Confidence Quotes which was the first of two confidence quote books. The other one is called "101 Confidence Quotes that will change your life" and contains more challenging and thought provoking quotes it will stop you in your tracks and make you question yourself and reflect on your past who you are today and who you can be tomorrow.

I have purposefully kept this book short and sweet so that you can get straight to the point. I hope that it inspires and challenges you and helps you to find the courage to step out of your shell, to leave the old you behind and become the person you know has been in hiding all of these years.

*

I believe this is a great book to keep with you and dip in and out of or read back to back in one sitting. However you choose to use it I hope it gives you what you have been looking for.

I would advocate reading some if not all of it daily because what you are trying to do is change your pathology, your way of thinking, to correct years of unhelpful patterns of relating to yourself and the world around you. Unfortunately those thoughts and feeling cannot be changed overnight but with some time practice and perseverance you can adopt and integrate a whole new way of being. Practice my friend does make perfect. So the more you read and repeat these quotes the easier it will be to integrate positive changes in your life.

If you don't want to carry a book around with you all the time then here are a few helpful hints to help you get the best out of the book.

- Once you have read the book why not write down one quote per day on a piece of paper and keep it with you making sure that you refer to it several times throughout the day.
- Write down the quotes that really speak to you on separate pieces of paper or card and leave them around the house/office/car where you will see them every day. By doing this you will unconsciously reinforce the positive message which will help to rewire your way of thinking.
- Record yourself saying them on your phone and listen to them every day. Remember repetition is the key.
- If you meditate you can use them as your daily mantra.

All I know is, from the feedback that I have received from the people who have bought this book on e-format it has helped them immensely so I know that it can help you in your life journey.

*

My philosophy is that you as an individual are responsible for everything that happens in your life and you are capable of making choices that are healthy and right for you. You have the power to do whatever you want. You do not have to be defined by what other people think of you. You do not have to live according to other peoples rules. You have the right to live according to your beliefs and carve out a life that you deserve to live. I know that you are all capable of setting healthy boundaries for yourselves you just have to have the confidence to put them in place and then maintain them. Even if you are in a situation right now where you don't have healthy boundaries with the help of this book you can create them and change your life. You can decide and define what is acceptable to you and YES it is OK to let other people know what you will not tolerate and even more importantly it is ok to say NO without feeling guilty.

With that being said I hope the following quotes allow you to tap into your inner strength to your creativity to your AWESOMENESS and start living life as the strong and confident person you are meant to be.

Much love Tony.

101 Quick and easy

Confidence Quotes.

*

1.

Don't lower your standards to make other people happy. Let them raise their standards to make you happy.

2.

The fastest way to feel GOOD about yourself is to stop thinking that you are BAD.

3.

Adversity is your best friend

because without it you will never

know how strong you truly are.

The more adversity you overcome the

stronger and more confident you will

feel.

4.

Sometimes life can be TOUGH.

But know that you are

TOUGHER.

5.

The greatest lesson you can ever teach

your children is to Love and Respect

themselves, the best way to teach them

how to do that is for you to Love and

Respect yourself!

6.

Can you remember who you were before

the world told you who you should be,

because that is who you were destined to

be. Find that person inside of you and set

them free.

7.

Whatever life throws at you throw it back

with a smile on your face.

8.

The world is your oyster and you are the

Pearl. Don't confine and define yourself

with limiting beliefs.

9.

Be your own HERO because by doing so

you are showing someone else how they

too can shine.

10.

Stop trying so hard to be somebody that

you are not. Instead focus all of that

energy into being more of who

YOU TRULY ARE.

11.

Never leave home without your keys,

your money and your CONFIDENCE.

12.

Just in case nobody has told you today

that you are incredible let me be the first

to say it. You are Incredible.

13.

Every time you say you cannot do

something you are telling the universe

that you do not deserve all the

splendours it is waiting to bestow upon

you. When life presents you with a

difficult situation it is giving you a gift in

disguise. Embrace it with open arms and

say thank you.

14.

Confidence is like a muscle, the more you

use it the stronger it gets.

15.

Find a reason to smile today and if you can't find a way to make someone else smile, that way your day will still have had meaning.

16.

Everybody has a calling, your job in life is to find that calling and live it.

17.

If you behave like a doormat then people will walk all over you.

18.

Fear of failure has moved out, it doesn't live here anymore. Confidence and Self-belief paid their deposit and they moved in yesterday.

19.

There are over 7 billion people on the planet but there is only ever going to be one of you and that sounds like a reason to celebrate your uniqueness and your individuality to me. Love and accept who you are right now this very minute.

20.

If you do not make a conscious effort to be who you want to be then you will be a combination of other people's ideas of what they think you should be.

21.

Remember this simple equation.

Thought + Belief + Action = You can do anything you set your mind to.

22.

Confidence is a state of mind. So ask yourself what state is your mind in?

23.

Start your day with something

incredible...

YOU.

24.

We make thousands of choices every day

without ever thinking about them. So

why not make one more choice and

choose to think

positively.

25.

There is only one person in this

world who can determine your

limitations and that's you.

Stop saying "I can't" and start saying

"I CAN"

26.

A smile is just as infections as the flu so

smile and spread love wherever you go

today.

27.

Emancipate yourself from negativity and

depression, say goodbye to it and

embrace joy and happiness because they

are both available to you at any time.

28.

When someone says to you "No you can't

do it" it doesn't mean that it can't be

done it just means they don't know how

to do it and they don't want you to do it

either. Trust your instincts and travel the

path that only you are meant to follow.

29.

The reason you have dreams is so that

you can follow them. Never give up.

30.

I have never had enough but always had

too much!

31.

Think of one thing you do well. Now do it

every day and watch your self-esteem sky

rocket.

32.

Never be afraid to say NO.

To speak your mind.

To voice your opinion.

To try something new.

To fall in love.

To trust your instincts.

To ask for what you need.

To believe in yourself because fear will paralyze you if you let it. Believe in yourself and just go for it.

33.

Every day is an opportunity to hit

the reset button and start again,

leave yesterday in the past and

focus on today, then repeat the

same process tomorrow.

34.

Life is a bitch now take it by the throat

and show it who is boss.

35.

We are all born with a unique purpose in

life. Just because other people haven't

found theirs don't let them distract you

from finding yours.

36.

When was the last time you looked in the

mirror and said "I am beautiful" Look in

the mirror and say it now. Excellent, now

say it again.

37.

Stop looking for excuses start looking for

reasons to excel.

38.

You don't need other people to like you

when you like yourself.

39.

In life the only person you really need to

impress is YOURSELF.

40.

The only way FORWARD is to stop looking

BACKWARDS.

41.

Laugh in the face of fear and follow your

dreams.

42.

You cannot change the past, but what

you do today will affect your tomorrow.

Start making today count towards your

future.

43.

Life is all about who you are today and

who you are going to be tomorrow, not

who you were yesterday.

44.

Once you have learned to truly love

yourself everything is easy and anything

is possible.

45.

Sometimes helping someone else is the

best way to help yourself.

If bad habits can become a routine then

so can good habits. Make a conscious

effort to do more of what you are good

at and what is good for you.

46.

The only time you truly fail is when you

never really try.

47.

If negative thoughts about ourselves

make us feel bad then surely positive

thoughts about ourselves can only make

us feel good. It's time to flip the script.

48.

If we never tried anything new or did

anything different we would never have

evolved. It is in our nature to explore and

grow so get off the sofa and start living

life, stop hiding from it.

49.

Life can be a rollercoaster. It has its ups and its downs, twists and turns but the important thing is to stay on for the ride until the end and enjoy every second of it.

50.

I am sure you have heard the saying "You are what you eat" well the same is true of your mind. "You are what you think" so it's important to throw out the negative programming and replace it with positivity and confidence.

51.

Fear can only control your life if you allow

it to have control.

52.

Dont give up. Don't give in. Keep trying.

Push yourself. Know that you can do it.

Believe in Yourself and you will make it.

53.

If you do what feels right for you then

there can be no wrong. Every experience

you have is a lesson waiting to be

learned.

54.

If you spend time worrying about all the things you cannot change then you will not have any time for the things you can change.

55.

When you are important to yourself you will become more important to other people. Remember you are your first priority.

56.

BE yourself because you can't BE anyone

else. Get comfortable in your skin and

accept yourself for who you are.

57.

Experience is the fastest route to success.

58.

Getting it wrong is the quickest way to

learn how to get it right.

59.

If you only do one thing today, make sure

it is to believe in yourself.

60.

Your life will not change unless you

change it.

61.

You are an accumulation of your

thoughts and actions. So if you want to

change your life, start with your thoughts

and follow through with your actions.

62.

Anything is POSSIBLE when you stop

believing it is IMPOSSIBLE.

63.

I am inspired to inspire - Sometimes the

best thing you can do for yourself is to do

something for someone else.

64.

Today is the day! But the day for what,

now that is up to you.

65.

Rejection is better than regret. It is better to try and fail than to live in fear of failure. You may not always get what you want but if you never try you are guaranteed to never get what you want.

66.

You are whoever you decide to be. It doesn't matter what title other people give you it is only important how you define yourself. Decide who you want to be and then be it.

67.

Every "failure" is a future success in

disguise.

68.

I will have a cocktail with a splash of

confidence, some self-esteem, two

fingers of positivity dusted in hope with a

cherry on top, two lumps of "I can do

anything" and a splash of self-respect, oh

and make it a double.

69.

Each person that you meet is an

opportunity to be an inspiration and

spread positivity and joy or you can make

them feel miserable and spread

negativity. What type of person do you

want to be?

70.

Your life is your own so live it by your

design. Don't let the influence of others

stop you from enjoying what is rightfully

yours.

71.

I am in control of my LIFE and my

DESTINY because I am in control of how I

think and what I do.

72.

When you stop judging and criticising

others you will be able to stop judging

and criticising yourself.

73.

Imagine if you could live in a world where

you never again said the words "Yes but"

think how different your life would be

and all that you could have achieved.

Replace "Yes but" with "I can" and

change your life forever, but remember

bad things may happen to you but that

doesn't mean that you have to react

negatively. Take a minute before reacting

and choose the most productive way

forward.

74.

Today I leave all negativity behind me

and walk with positivity in my pocket.

75.

It is better to fail in attempting something

than to be successful at trying nothing.

76.

We all experience Hard times but that is

so we can truly appreciate the good

times. Every cloud has a silver lining and

tomorrow is another day.

77.

If you fill your head with positive

thoughts then there can be no room left

for the negative ones.

78.

Be your own motivation. Let your dreams

push you forward, don't let them hold

you back

79.

If you subtract the T from the phrase "I

Can't" you are left with "I Can" and those

two words will change your life forever.

80.

Never hide

your light

so that

someone

else can

shine.

*

81.

Instead of being a victim of your

circumstances, be the VICTOR of your

circumstances. Take responsibility and be

in control of your life.

82.

A big part of building your confidence

comes from facing your fear and doing

the thing that scared you. Repetition is

the key. Do it and do it again until it

becomes easy.

83.

If you believe you have no limitations

then in life you will not be limited. Push

yourself to exceed and reap the rewards.

84.

The power to be whatever you want to

be is within you. You just have to find

that power and let it out.

85.

In order to be outstanding you just have

to be yourself.

86.

Nothing is impossible unless you believe

it is impossible.

87.

Forgiveness will only make you a better

person. Holding on to anger makes you a

bitter person.

88.

Everything happens for a reason even

when you don't know what the reason is.

Have faith and believe in yourself. You

are stronger than you think.

89.

If something needs to change in your life

then there is a good chance that what

needs to change is YOU. Look at yourself

before you start looking at other people's

problems and imperfections.

90.

The greatest change you can make in the

world is to change yourself.

~

91.

Nobody has the power to lower your

confidence or self-esteem unless you

give them the power to do it. Stand

strong and stay true to yourself.

92.

Confidence is like a bird.

When you set it free

it will truly soar.

*

93.

Do not be restricted by age, race,

religion, sex, sexuality, height, weight or

colour. The only way you should ever be

limited is by the extent of your

imagination.

94.

I believe that we are born with limitless

potential but over time we build blocks

and barriers that get in the way. All we

have to do is remove those blocks to

uncover our true greatness.

95.

You are PERFECT just the way you are. Do not change to make other people happy.

96.

Positive thinking is good - positive action is amazing.

97.

Obstacles are put in our way to see if what we want is really worth fighting for, don't give up at the first hurdle, if you want to succeed you must keep going.

98.

Just because today may have been a

terrible day that doesn't mean tomorrow

won't be the best day of your life. You

never know what is around the corner.

Have faith.

99.

I may not be where I want to be in life

but at least I am not where I used to be.

Make every day a step closer to where

you want to be in life.

100.

In order to truly love

someone else

you must first

be able to love

YOURSELF.

101.

It's easy to be POSITIVE. Just stop being

NEGATIVE. It's a choice and the choice is

yours.

*

Bonus Quotes.

1.

There are no mistakes in life, only lessons

that are waiting to be learned.

2.

I accept myself for who I am and I am

confident at a core level.

3.

Believe and trust in yourself. It is the

most rewarding thing you will ever do.

4.

It wasn't my intention to be this amazing

I was just born that way.

5.

Why spend time focusing on things you

can't change when you can spend that

time on things you can change?

6.

Try, try and try again and if that doesn't

work, try some more.

7.

You can make a mistake once but if you

make the same mistake twice – that's a

choice.

8.

Every day is an opportunity to be a better

version of who you were yesterday.

9.

There are 1,440 minutes in a day. How

many do you use to make your dreams

come true?

10.

Wear your confidence like a bullet proof

vest and refuse to let any negativity get

to you today.

11.

Being yourself is the best person you

could be. Stop trying to be what others

expect you to be.

12.

Other people say MISTAKE. I say

OPPORTUNITY.

13.

Sometimes the hardest things in life are

the greatest lessons. Say thank you to the

tough times because they made you who

you are today.

14.

Repeat after me. "I am the creator of my

own destiny and I am responsible for

everything that happens in my life"

15.

When you stop trying you start dying.
(scary thought huh)never give up, you
deserve better.

16.

The only thing that should blend in is
your makeup.

17.

Life is like a jigsaw but when you have
confidence and believe in yourself all the
pieces come together to create a perfect
picture.

18.

The hard truth of it is you cannot always

control what happens in your life, the

only thing you can control is your attitude

towards what happened and the choices

you make in responding to it. Never

forget you are in control of your life. It is

all on you.

19.

Repeat your successes and not your

failures.

20.

In the immortal words of Britney Spears

"You better work Bitch" because

anything worth having will only come

with hard work and that includes your

confidence. If you want it you have got to

earn it.

*

Thank you for reading 101 Quick and Easy

Confidence Quotes, but that isn't it, just for you I

have added the first 5 Quotes from 101

Confidence Quotes that will change your life.

101

Confidence Quotes

That will change your life.

1.

Right now, this very second you are the best that you can be because you cannot be anything other than what you are. Celebrate yourself. Love yourself. Respect yourself. Accept yourself. Trust yourself. Have faith in yourself and know that you are a good person.

2.

Greatness is achieved by overcoming challenges and by pushing yourself to do things you didn't know that you could do but believed in yourself enough to try.

Remember nothing rewarding ever came without effort. Try and if that doesn't work try again, then try harder. Remember that you are worth the effort.

3.

You are the living embodiment of Ultimate Hope, Pure Love and Infinite Possibilities. You can do anything when you apply yourself and have faith in your abilities. Never give up. Never back down. Stay strong and know that you can do it.

4.

If you follow someone else's path you will end up at their destination. Follow your dreams; listen to where your heart is calling you to go. Enjoy your journey and find your own destination, you owe it to yourself to fulfil the destiny that is rightfully yours.

5.

I have found that the people who accuse you of being selfish are only doing so because you are not doing what they want when they want in the way they want you to do it and if that makes you selfish then so be it because really they are the ones who are being selfish for expecting you to meet their demands and needs ahead of your own. Don't feel guilty, don't feel bad about yourself instead realise that they are trying to manipulate you for their own interests, to fulfil their needs; they are not concerned by what you want or need, so ask yourself who is being selfish and who is letting who down?

If you have enjoyed 101 Quick and Easy Confidence Quotes you may also enjoy my affirmations book called 101 "I AM" Power affirmations.

It covers the main areas in life such as Love, Success, Responsibility, Health, Confidence and more.

Here are a few selected affirmations to give you a feel for the book. I hope you like them.

"I AM confident in my relationships, I set healthy boundaries and I AM able to speak my mind and voice my opinion without fear of rejection"

"I AM a good person and I appreciate all that I am and all that I will ever be"

I AM a success in all that I do because I approach everything with openness honesty and sincerity"

"I AM grateful for all that the universe bestows upon me and I know that everything that comes to me does so at the right time in the right way"

"I AM in control of what I eat and I only eat healthy food that nourishes my mind and my body"

"I AM awash with love because it fills and flows through me every day"

In this book I also explain the various ways you can use affirmations and how to get the most from them. I also talk about negative affirmations and how to correct years of negative programming.

Once again all the affirmations are original and written by me and not available anywhere else.

All books are also available in e-format.

Tony T Robinson

101 Quick and Easy Confidence Quotes.

Printed in Great Britain
by Amazon